MW01601348

I No Longer Hold the Hand That Held Me Down

By
Brandie
Brace

Copyright © 2024 Brandie Brace White
Copyright Â© 2025 Brandie Brace White
All rights reserved.

First printing: April 2024
Second edition printing: February 2025

ISBN: 978-1-967131-00-6

Published by Novelle Publishing, LLC

NOVELLE PUBLISHING

I No Longer

Hold the Hand

that

Held

Me

Down

I have written since I was a child. I loved it. I loved words. There was a time when words betrayed me. There was a time when I couldn't write anything, because I was not the same girl that was so eloquent in her youth. Two things happened that brought me out of the coma. I got divorced. I made friends with two of the most incredible and supportive people I have known. They carried me through the disaster and showed me how much of that young girl I forgot existed.

I married young, not too young, but young enough that I had no comprehension of what a lifetime relationship meant. We both had flaws. We both broke promises and we both failed each other. I won't place blame on either of us. I should have been stronger. I didn't know myself back then. Looking back though, I wouldn't change anything. One choice, one slight misstep of my past and I wouldn't be here. I wouldn't be the person I am now, and I like who I am now. Sure, maybe, I could have been here long ago if I had made different choices, but the experience that led up to this place is one I wouldn't trade for a hundred second chances.

My friends and family have been the greatest inspiration in my life. There are a lot of positive influence and some negative. I have found that I always learned more from those bad choices because those are the opportunities for us to decide what kind of a life we want.

I used to think that people are nefarious creatures at their base. That some hid it better than others, and some overcame that nature easier than others. But I believed that all people had it in them to be immoral, disreputable, selfish, degenerate and really just bad. The degree to which people impose that nature on others is the question I thought needed to be explored and answered. Looking back now, I think that people are lost at their base. We are all just searching for the path that will feel right, that won't hurt or won't hurt as much. Sometimes that search makes us into something we really didn't want to be. When people say, "That isn't the real you... you aren't this decrepit creature you are acting like," that really isn't true. It IS you; it is the you that you have allowed yourself to become. But it isn't the you that you are stuck with. I recently heard the analogy of the caterpillar and the butterfly told in a different way. Everyone always talks about the butterfly like the caterpillar was transformed into something new and ceased being that furry, crawly, creepy slithering creature. The physiology is that the caterpillar was always, also, the butterfly. Everything the butterfly needs to have beautiful wings and strong antennae are already part of the caterpillar. The caterpillar just needed the opportunity to let it out. That new perspective spoke volumes to me. It seems that you don't have to do anything to transform who you are. You just have to let those beautiful parts of you out. All of that good is inside you too, right along with the bad and it's up to us to decide who gets the main stage in our lives.

So... where has your search led you? Is it someplace safe? Is it someplace, right? Or are you still looking for your path? Is there someone holding you back from finding the you that you could be, are they holding you down? How long will you let them? And here is the biggest question: IS IT YOU?

Do you hold yourself to goals that you would never dream of holding others to? Do you blame others for losing your way? Are you postponing a change because you are afraid of what you don't know the change will bring? How long will you hold you down?

I sincerely hope you enjoy the pages that follow. There is no expectation that you can identify with every snippet or story, but I hope that you find something in these pages that helps you, strengthens you, encourages you and allows you to break the bonds that hold you down.

To all of you on the battle to break those bonds, this book is dedicated to you. Be curious, ask questions, reflect and observe. These are the keys to happiness.

Contents

ACKNOWLEDGMENTS

There are many folks to mention here and if I tried to name them all, I am afraid I would miss someone and never forgive myself. I will say this – to everyone who encouraged me even when and especially when I felt like I lost my voice, Thank You.

None of this I have now or what I will have later would be possible without you.

THE RUN

"A moment of choice is a moment of truth..."
Steven Covey

It was a cool morning; 6 a.m. The air was crisp
with a hint of humidity coming from the fog
vanishing as the sun rose. She looked out the open
window to her backyard and took it in. The city is
in the distance, waking up with a gradual hum as
cars begin to scatter the streets. There was a
division of trees, green space, wildflower gardens
and shrubs that stretched from the city limits to
the edge of a housing edition. It was part of a
partnership project to preserve natural areas,
increase green spaces and provide an extension of
the suburbs closer to the city. The project
encouraged housing developers to keep as much
of the land in its natural state in exchange for tax
and labor subsidies. The result of this agreement
led to a planned neighborhood of new homes
surrounded by the effect of a mature space.
However, the tradeoff for this special kind of
construction is that the only entry by car to the
subdivision from the city was by highway. For
avid runners, there was a nature trail that
connected the subdivision to the municipal park
nestled on the edge of the city limits. The trail had

originally been a back entrance for construction vehicles as the houses were being built. After the they were finished, the developers, in accordance with the project objectives, planted new trees and wildflowers to return the area to its original state.

She had picked the subdivision because it was close enough to the city, she could drive there in less than a half hour- even in traffic, but she chose the street because it was on the outer edge of the neighborhood and the paved markers behind her backyard led to the newly renovated nature trails. She enjoyed a weekend run on the trails that extended 3.1 miles to convene with the city park. Full circle run, including a ring around the park was 7.4 miles, took her about an hour and a half, and it was a nice reward on a Saturday morning. A reward for the week was just what she needed.

There was so much to do today, and she really needed time to unwind before the hubbub started this evening. Running always cleared her mind; relieved her stress. Work had been so crazy these last few weeks with her last case. The trial date was moved up and it made the preparation even more rushed than it would have been with her other case load.

Her friend from college, Sandy, was having a party tonight to celebrate her recent engagement to an up-and-coming junior associate in a very prestigious marketing firm. The couple was just nearly perfect. Sandy went to a top twenty college, but never really expected to use her education except to make polite, interesting conversation to nab a man, which she did in her third year. Now after several years of courting, they were ready to take the plunge.

Engagement... that is a word not likely to grace her vocabulary these days. There was no time for a relationship. Maybe a few that she could possibly have seen a future with, but that was a long time ago. She made choices - law school, internships, clerk assignments and finally, a chance to become a partner at the firm. These were the things that were important to her. She just wasn't wired the same way as her friends. It was okay, she had reconciled the decisions with herself. She had no immediate family still living, so there was no one waiting for grandkids. This was the life she wanted - sure, sometimes there is a wonder, a daydream of something different. But this is where she was, and she had all she wanted.

Her mental to-do list for the day grew with the engagement party tonight, she needed to wrap the gift and oh, – pick up her dress from the cleaners. The last time she wore that dress was when the firm hosted a cocktail evening for a prospective client. The dress was simple and elegant, and it does well for most formal events. It was her "go-to" dress for parties; she didn't have time to think too hard about her attire. It'll do.

The grass needed cut and the weeds needed pulled from her garden out back – it has gotten overrun since the work overload – she would do that when she got home or maybe she would ask the neighbor's boy if he would like the job. The neighbor mentioned to her just the other day that the boy was looking for some ways to make extra money for a new bike. The boy was only 10... or 11... she wasn't exactly sure, but she knew he only stood about as tall as her shoulders, so she guessed at his age. That was the fairer option. She had no desire to fiddle with the yard this weekend. Normally, she would appreciate a day to soak up the sun and get some exercise in the garden, but this weekend was going to be a busy one. The neighbor's boy would be the perfect solution – win-win all around.

If that wasn't enough, she needed to run through some documents this afternoon to get her next week in order since she knew she wouldn't feel like it tomorrow. She had lost some alcohol tolerance since college. Cocktail hour for her is a few sips of a chardonnay, smiles, handshakes and home in bed by 10 p.m. or, more accurately, home working until midnight. If she has a few real drinks, she is certain she will be laid up all day with a hangover and she knew she wasn't going to escape a couple of "engagement shots" with her friend. No one really knows how old they are getting until they try to have a few drinks like they are in their college days again. She has prepared her exit line, so it isn't a total disaster.

So much to do.... She needed this. She needed some time to herself...just an hour or so. She stepped outside the French doors, to her patio, locked the door behind her, and tucked the key in the zipper pocket of her sweatshirt. She knelt on the patio step to tighten the laces again. The low hum of the city was muffled by the trees that were strewn through the neighborhood. She nearly skipped across the natural rock walk she had laid from the patio to the rear of her yard and out the back gate that led to the subdivision trail. She could see the entrance to the connecting path in the short distance and headed out walking in that direction for a little warm up.

This morning – this Saturday – the pavement beneath her feet pounded with an odd echo as she got closer to the trail entrance. She noticed it. She explained to herself that she just hadn't been out for a few days, and it was still very early; no one was out and about yet.

When she got to the trail, she finally wound a thick brown band around her golden locks and bent down to stretch before she got started. She was naturally slim. In high school, she discovered with some despair that slim — skinny — is not always desirable. No curves. It seemed exercise was the key to bulk those bird legs into something men found attractive. Again, she did not mind. She enjoyed the benefit of exercise not just for her body, but for the cleansing of her mind and the distraction that often crept in and misaligned her focus. She was an extremely focused person, with some pride in it as well.

She set off, admiring the leaves on the trees that were green and full of life. It was the middle of summer and the temperatures had been unseasonably cool. She appreciated the slight chill this early in the morning. It made the run more pleasurable with the crisp air. She let her mind clear as she took in the little patch of nature around her.

She was halfway to the city. A faint odor of exhaust hung in the air battling the fresh green smells of the nature trail of which she was nearing the end. The sun had climbed and took with it the layer of cloudiness. Tiny animals — squirrels, rabbits, birds — had made a home in the man-made wilderness. She could hear them rustle about the tall grass and wild shrubs set just off the paved path. She picked up the pace when she could see more of the tops of the buildings over the tops of trees. She loved the air that snapped her face as she ran down the path. She still couldn't quite shake the list of activities of the day in her head. She tried to shift her focus to the run, steady the pace, but the distraction was hard to fight today.

As she came closer to the park entrance, she toyed with the idea of taking a cab back home. If she did, she would have the time to finish everything on her to-do list and then she may stop stressing and enjoy her time. Settled, cab it is. Now she relaxed a little. She jogged through the open gate of the park and curved around the outside track that encompassed the medium sized park. She had finally lost herself in the run; no wonder she didn't see them at first.

The shouting shook her from her errant thoughts. She stopped in mid stride, landing on both feet almost as precisely as if she had jumped in place. She could tell that they were arguing. An affair, is that what she heard…a child too, maybe? She couldn't quite make it out, but whoever they were, she was an intruder in their private moment and it might be better if they didn't know she was there. She ducked off the track, into the hedge that bordered the park. The couple was to her left and a bit ahead of her — about 50 feet. It was a wonder they didn't hear her coming too, but then again, they were preoccupied and equally distracted from their surroundings.

She was alone in the park - outside of the couple - as far as she could tell. It was early, she admitted to herself, but surely there would be a few more people coming around soon and that eased her mind a little regarding her intrusion.

She got antsy in the shrubs as she half-listened to their argument; at best, she estimated she had been there about eight minutes. She thought of easing out of her hidey hole and continuing on her way, but then, that would definitely be noticeable now, and how would she explain why she had been crouched in a bush in the first place? She never should have stopped. She should have just kept going and ignored whatever was going on over there. She was so startled; she just hid on instinct. Flight or fight or... hide? So, she waited. It had been nearly fifteen minutes. Her head finally took over, what was the difference between her hiding in a bush and them screaming in the park? Both equally odd situations neither party would like to explain, so there was little risk she would be asked to do it. As she gathered herself to leave her refuge, she noticed the disagreement seemed to have gotten worse, although the volume of their voices had lessened considerably. They were face to face, talking low right into each other's mouths.

The evolution of the argument felt a little alarming and she decided it was not the time to leave her protective brush, but then, as quickly as it had escalated, it seemed to diffuse. The couple embraced; the man's hands rubbed the woman's back gently as they glided over its surface. She sighed relief…now she watched curiously at the lovers as the man kissed the woman softly, cupping her face in his hands. It was over finally, and she could get back on her run with little time lost. She smiled, partly at her own embarrassment and partly at the lovers' ending quarrel. The man's hands slid down the woman's neck now as their lips pulled apart. From such a distance, she could see the confused look on the woman's face as the man's grip grew tighter around her neck. She shrunk back into the hedge quickly, quietly, still barely hidden by the greenery and her stomach was turning flips wondering what she should do now. The woman, with very little noise, was squirming and shaking and then it was over. The man dropped her like a sack of dirty laundry on the ground. The man looked around frantically, hurriedly, and then she heard his quick steps clack down the path past her. She waited again… stunned… speechless… thoughtless…what just happened. She could no longer hear the man's footsteps. She was relieved again, grateful even to have the ordeal done. But was it done? The woman lay lifeless nearly 50 feet away. Wait, was the woman lifeless? She only saw the woman drop to the ground. Right, the man was strangling her, it looked like, but how could she tell for sure? She was nearly 50 feet away. Maybe the woman just passed out. She peered through the spaces in the bush in the woman's direction. Still no movement. The woman looked like a human pretzel. She waited several more minutes. The park was silent; it had only been less than ten minutes, despite the eternity that had just passed. Still no movement. She looked down at the dirt beneath her knees. The shrub had become too familiar to her now. A quiet came over her, immobilizing her body and mind. The minute that passed felt static.

Cautiously, deliberately, she crept out from the bush and stood slowly. She looked around as nonchalantly as she could and took a first step down the path. Within seconds she was jogging again, and she reached the smaller gate on the northeast side of the park. She paused slightly, after exiting the gate and crossed the street. She made her way four blocks east, away from the park to the intersection of Sixth and Hoover. Her hand flung in the air, independent of her body. The taxi's brakes squealed as it came to a slow stop and turned off his light, signifying he was taking on a passenger.

"2973 Summer Trail Drive," she spoke without inflection.

"Got it, ma'am," the cabby replied, "no other stops in the city? That will be at least a 30-minute haul with the highways as they are this morning."

"No stops. 2973 Summer Trail Drive," she maintained a lifeless tone as she stared vacantly out the backseat window as the cab pulled onto Hoover and headed toward the highway.

There was a lot to do today. And she still needed to make it to the cleaners before the party.

STILL

it is one of those days when you wake early without
even trying.

you writhe and blink like a newborn from a long nap.

the Sun seeps through the gap in the curtain; no one
is awake.

the aroma of coffee opens your eyes as it fills the cup

a playful breeze blows outside, rustling the leaves to a
whirlwind.

it is so quiet; you can hear the chain of the Tree
swing.

everything and nothing exist at once – you are in the
center of it.

you feel the gentle wind as a lover caressing your neck.

the sweet calm Isolates you in a warm cocoon.

revel in this scarce luxury just a moment more, until –

it starts as a soft noise and grows stronger.

Little feet clumsily plopping down the stairs.

sweet, small voice through the silence pulls you from that peaceful retreat.

a face – as bright as the Sun that first greeted you – grins at the sight of you.

your eyes smile back, and you know your true peace: it's in her Laughter.

FUTURE

Glass bulbs colored by rainbows and sweat bob
Over the reflecting pool.
The boy sits in silence –
Almost an eerie reverence – on the bench,
looking out.

A boy sitting there. My boy. The flowers in
bloom in the gardens
Surrounding; the sun shines down to reveal its
twin in the water.
He sits, thinking, wondering, waiting…

What dreams does he dream of sitting there
alone? What he will
Do when he's older, what he will do tomorrow.
Just sitting there
On the concrete bench, looking out.

The day was perfect. A trip to the gardens, a
summer
Get-away for the day. A mother that caught a
special glimpse of her son
When we paused by the pool.

He is a great artist, a great writer, a great kid. He has big goals,
Big plans, big purpose. Whatever he thinks of he creates –
In ink or in pencil – it comes to life.

It is so peaceful here. Just the water, the sun, the flowers.
The bulbs still mingle with the lily pads
So naturally, it's like they were always there.

UNEXPECTED MOMENTS

CRASH.

Is this real?
I faintly hear sirens; see the halos of the lights
But the rest is a blur.
Closer, closer now, I hear them – yes, it's real.
Liquid rainbows ooze across the black asphalt.
Beads of glass gather in puddles of shimmer.
Steam rises in hurried, deliberate slivers like a
teapot ready to be poured.

FLASH.

Is this real?
I remember pulling from the drive like it was a
dream.
Now, I am here, dazed and sitting behind a
deflated bag.
Face in my hands, numb in my heart.
Was I distracted…of course I was.
The fight was overwhelming this time.
His face was cruel, his words unforgivable.
It's all I could think of…

SIGH.

Crews arrive; assess the damage.
It only feels worse than it is.
Get out. Inspect the car; others are much worse.
At a glance, just pop out the dents and a new
light is all I need.

But underneath, the frame is bent; the axle is
broken.
And this I cannot yet see. I suspect that a drive
or two will prove the damage there
Is well beyond repair.

MILE MARKER 139
PROLOGUE

The paper-thin walls of the tiny cabin shook at the force of the wind outside. She wrestled her baby boy into a fresh diaper and sleeper. She hoped she could get the baby to bed before – and if – he came back. He had been gone since Thursday night. She knew that meant he was on a bender, probably in the next town over. Monday, the work week started, and he would be coming home for a change of clothes, at least. Three days seemed to be the longest reprieve she ever got from his mood swings.

Both were only seventeen when she got pregnant. Their parents wanted them to finish school and see where they were. In a small town like Aurora, finishing school would have only meant they were "educated" and pregnant. They still weren't going anywhere.

The two of them settled that they would make their own life; why not? They were in love like no other seventeen-year-old in their class. So, they dropped out. He landed a job at the ethanol plant working second shift. In the mornings, he tended to the pastures and the cattle on Mr. Kramer's land. Ranch work had made him strong. He had a broad chest, cut shoulders and abdominals despite the booze gut he worked so hard for. His thick, black curly hair was long on top. He kept it slicked back most of the time, unless he was on a bender and then it hung to one side, the curls covering his face a bit, but letting his deep, dark eyes show through. Those were the eyes that frightened her. She seemed so frail in comparison. Her small frame was thin, with their meager income, she often did without for her family. Her face was sunken, and her eyes darkened by her sacrifice, but her smile made her beautiful and the kindness in her voice made her warm. Her golden hair was long and straight. She brushed it every night after the baby went to sleep. Then she waited for him. Sometimes hopeful for him to show her a sign of his love, sometimes worrisome for him to come home.

Mr. Kramer let them rent the broken-down cabin at the back of his plot for pennies a month on account of the part-time cattle hand he was getting from the deal. The problem was, lately, it was *too* part-time. The cabin was nice enough. Unfinished wood floors, threadbare curtains faded by years and sunshine. Four rooms: kitchen, two bedrooms, living room and a tiny bathroom replaced the outhouse almost thirty years ago. It was a place they would call home, for now.

After she got the baby down, she sat in the wooden rocker in the center of the living room. She slowly pushed her foot against the worn rug that covered the floor swaying her and the chair slightly. She was putting the day to bed in her mind. Her gaze landed on the picture that rested on the mantle of the fireplace that heated their tiny abode. She smiled silently for a second at the thought of her first love. They knew each other since they were in grade school, of course, Aurora is a very small town. It was the start of their junior year and a pep rally for homecoming. She was a peppy cheerleader and he set his sights on her. He made her feel like she was the most beautiful woman in the world. She felt special when she walked down the sidewalk in town holding his hand. People smiled at them and nodded, and she just knew they were thinking about what a lovely couple they made and how happy they would make each other. That is what she was thinking anyway. They were happy together. In the Fall, they went on the town hayride and went pumpkin picking. The two were inseparable. They felt like they could conquer the world. At Christmas, when they figured out she was expecting, he was supportive, kind. He promised her that he would take care of her. Defied his parents and so did she because they were so sure that the life they could make together was better than the one their parents tried to convince them to take. And it was true, he did take care of her, at first, maybe…?

Reality came back and stole her smile again. So much had changed in him over that short year and a half. She noticed some of the gradual changes, less small talk at the end of the day; less of his gentle touch when he left her in the morning. She could sometimes see the disdain in his eyes as they shared dinners together. Now, when the baby cried, he scoffed and took his meal in the bedroom to finish so as not to be disturbed. His benders had become more frequent. Mr. Kramer was getting impatient with his excuses. He had always told her that he wanted her to stay home with the baby. But the last few times he came home, there was such disgust with the house, with the baby, with her, she often wondered if she should get a job and try to help support him. When he hit her, he always said she should help him more. Once, about a month after the baby was born, he went out celebrating and didn't come home for 5 days. She assumed this was how it went with new parents, and they were so young, she had no frame of reference. When he came back early in the morning, his rage nearly sent her back to the hospital. She was lucky that Mr. Kramer had come by to get him for work.

The horn of Kramer's old Chevy was the closest thing to an angel coming to her rescue. Then after work, he was so attentive to the baby and to her. So apologetic and remorseful and even tried to stay on the wagon to keep things together. But now, over a year later, the stress seems to have won him over. Was this just a phase that he would come out of, and he would be thankful that she was so loyal to him? Could she risk it if it wasn't a phase?

She heard the rumble of his truck coming up the dirt road towards the cabin and her stomach began to churn. She knew it was his, because he had removed part of the muffler to make the truck have an awful growl. He thought it was youthful and dangerous. She could hear the music from the truck blaring and could tell he was trying to shut down the engine. She arose slowly from the rocker, unsure what to think. He seemed to be making more of a scene than usual after he came back from drinking. Something was different, darker as she tried to look out the window without being seen. She could only make out silhouettes in the moonlight. The door of the truck opened, but never closed. She could hear him tumble out of the truck, cursing as he hit the dirt. She felt a trigger in her soul as she heard him stumbling through the gate, tripping on the water hose and cursing more. She was frozen in her step as he called to her from the yard. The sarcasm and hatred hung in his words. She heard a shotgun cock. Instantly, alarms rang inside her head, her eyes swelled so much that she could barely see through the cloudiness of her tears. Her inherent instinct – her son. She sprinted to his tiny room in three steps. He had stirred from the commotion but was still in a state of sleepiness. A wicker basket of diapers, wipes, lotions and powders sat on the floor by the crib. She dumped it quickly and lined it with blankets. She could still hear his voice; berating and gruff and she could hear him pissing on the sidewalk that led to the door, singing and shouting at her. He hadn't fired the gun yet, maybe she was overreacting.

However, she could not risk the minutes she had in case she wasn't. She scooped up the small boy onto her chest and nestled him in the basket, covering him with blankets. She slid the window up quietly and quickly, thanking the stars that the baby's room was at the back of the house, and she could slip away unnoticed. There was a small state highway about a half mile from the cabin, through the woods that surrounded the tiny house and then through a field of tall grass for the cattle to graze. If only she could make it there, maybe she could flag down a car and she could get away. They could get away. She lowered the basket out the window carefully until it reached the ground, then climbed out herself. She must take great care not to alert him in his stupor that she was not in the house. She crept toward the cover of the trees that lined the back of the cabin. The trees, she hoped, would provide the shield she needed.

A shot rang out. She didn't know yet if he was in the house or if he had accidentally fired the gun. She had hardly made it into the darkness she aimed for, but the shot didn't slow her pace. He must have gone into the house and didn't find them there. That was it because now she could hear him shout louder and more furious. She was past the trees now and into the field. He knows she isn't there. If he knows she is gone, he knows the boy is gone and her escape is futile. She kept running, the basket jostling on her arm and the baby was crying now. There might be no hope for them. Wait. She could see the lights of a car in the short distance. She ran even faster now, if that was possible. What if she couldn't reach the highway in time – the shotgun fired again, louder, echoing in her head like a gong. She cleared the fields and could see the road; she could see the headlights, still two specks of light in the blackness. Her heart was broken. The next seconds seemed like a lifetime. They were too far away. The car was too far away. She looked down at her baby, fussing, confused and frightened by the sounds of the gunfire. She could hear him shouting. She knew he had figured out where she went, and he was coming closer. Too much to risk. A hot tear made a path down her cheek as she crouched down to the asphalt and gently placed the basket clear of the yellow line and draped a bright yellow blanket over the handle. She touched her lips with two fingers and reached for her son. She turned slowly toward the house. The moon was full and the light of it streamed through the clouds and shone a path through the sky to the tiny cabin. She had taken refuge there - a quiet place for her and her boy. She had been beaten down there. A horrid prison that kept her bound. She looked down once more at the basket and then ran towards the woods as quickly as she ran from them. It took only seconds until she disappeared in the thick darkness. Somewhere in the field of tall grass, the shot rang out. A pause, then a masculine cry before the final shot ended the terror. The clouds moved into one another, and the stream of moonlight faded into black over the tiny cabin.

A mixture of country twang and static was low on the radio. "John – John? Are you listening to me? I think we missed our turn…"

"No, Mary, I am not listening. Did you hear that? It sounded like fireworks or…" John's eyes scanned the sky for any sign of festive light but found none. He instinctively slowed as he searched and when his eyes met the road again, he saw it; something by the road maybe, and a dark figure running from it. It was too far away to be sure. Maybe thirty seconds or so and he pulled to the side until he could make it out…a basket? He stepped out of the car apprehensively and moved closer to it. John could make out the sounds now. Two gun shots fired close to one another. Then he heard the cry from beneath the blankets.

SNOW

Into everyone's life, a little snow must fall.

        The streets and the walks are littered,

           By dirt and trash and grime.

But when the snow falls down, they are
Cleansed, somehow, by a blanket of bright, fresh
white.

It is the same with our lives

          When they are littered

        By hurt and stress and grief.

So, welcome the snow,
that sometimes falls slow,
To wash all the litter away.

SHAM

What inspires the flower to soak up the sun

To drink from the rain and spread through the meadows?

What inspires the bird to nest in the trees to

Hatch her young and then spill them from safety to fly on their own?

What inspires the wolf to howl at the moon,
To run in a pack, and mate for life?

What inspires the planet to swing around the sun,
Erupt with fire and quake so fiercely?

What inspires the meek to be hopeful,
The proud to be angry?

What inspires the honest to be optimistic,
The deceitful to be leery?

What inspires them – can it inspire me?

THE MUSE

The knock at the door made Paul's head shake. He opened his eyes reluctantly and squeezed them shut as the sharp rays of the mid-morning sun shone through the plate glass windows. He laid still in his king size bed, and listened to the persistent and consistent knock. Paul had no intention of getting up yet. He opened his eyes again, ready to face the light intruding on his slumber. "I really should have closed the drapes last night," he thought to himself. Paul rolled over on his side, away from the unforgiving rays and noticed multiple missed calls and messages on his cell phone – all from Bas. Paul's head was clearing now and he noticed the knocking had stopped. He picked up his cell just as it was ringing again. "Oh, hey Bas," he was indifferent and still gruff from sleep.

"Dad! What in the hell is wrong with you, it is almost eleven in the morning, you don't answer your phone, you don't answer your door??" Basil's jaw tightened as he spoke, his words edged with quiet frustration.

"Well, I guess that mystery is solved," Paul muttered, "I am here, I am fine, I had a late night that's all." His voice was stronger now, and he was a little cross that his son was checking up on him. "Are you still at the door? Should I let you in?" Paul was oozing sarcasm now.

Bas softened a bit, "Maybe you should just give me a key, but yeah, I am still here, come let me in."

Paul's routine had become robotic once he got out of bed. Something had to ground him, so he found that structure in the little things. He reached for a tee shirt to match his pajama pants, slipped on his house moccasins and headed toward the door. His bedroom was at the back of his spacious New York apartment; spacious because he bought the neighboring unit and combined and renovated the space to accommodate his growing family. That was in the years of plenty, when his art was moving through the gallery doors faster than he could create it. When he was taking orders and working in binges while Peg ran the house, did the school drop off and PTA. She was his hero; she was the best person he had known and she brought out the best parts of him. Peg. These years without her felt like he didn't know himself anymore. Peg kept a garden on the rooftop of their New York apartment building. She grew spices and root vegetables, and the other tenants didn't mind, of course, because she shared her crops. In the summer, you could catch the fragrance of sage, oregano, sweet basil, and lavender as it wafted down to the street in front of their building. She loved gardening, growing things, making things. Peg was an artist herself in so many mediums, creating something from nothing.

Their kids' names, for example, allowed space for Peg's affinity for plants and her creativity gifted them with unique names. Paul didn't mind, there wasn't much that she couldn't convince him of when she wanted. Basil was the youngest. Jasmine - Minnie for short - and June, of course, was familiar for Juniper. Minnie came early and she was the oldest, ruling the roost with her siblings. June was a typical middle child, going with the flow. Both the girls had launched careers early in the same creative vane as their parents. Minnie opened a resale shop where she refinished furniture in Avante Garde style adding her unique touch. June was an illustrator, inheriting her father's gift of art. Bas went in a more corporate direction, but his real gift was people. He had a knack for knowing what people needed and finding a way to give it to them – something he picked up from his mom, no doubt.

Bas was standing in the broad hallway outside Paul's apartment door. An overnight bag slung over his shoulder, a lightweight jacket in hand and a ball cap rough around the edges of the bill. He took the look of his mother, sandy blonde hair and soft green eyes. His chin was his father's, but his tenacity, his mother's. Bas looked at his dad up and down as he opened the door, evaluating his build and his face to make sure he was eating and sleeping - it didn't look like he was getting enough of either.

The two shared an embrace, patting each

other on the back and giving a little shake to their shoulders before separating. Paul pulled Bas's overnight bag into the entry. "I love to see you son, but what are you doing here? You aren't due back for a couple more weeks, I thought?" Paul's face was curious when he asked and he continued through the entry hall and led Bas to the kitchen to start on some breakfast, or lunch maybe.

Basil's fiancée, Anna, scored her dream job last year in Seattle, as a communications lead for a growing media start up. He worked out an arrangement with his investment firm to work from Seattle and make monthly trips to the New York office for check-ins and schmoozing some of his top local clients. This made for some non-traditional working hours with the time zone difference, but they made it work.

"It's been three weeks since I have been here, Dad," Basil's expression grew a little more alarmed. Could his dad have lost track of that much time? He knew that since his mom passed, it was harder and harder to get his dad out of the house, to see friends or go out to eat dinner, and impossible to go to any of his old gallery haunts. But this time was different, Paul seemed unconcerned by the lapse of time he'd missed. Paul looked at Bas, nodded and continued to putter around the kitchen, looking for bread to toast to match the eggs he'd already pulled from the fridge. "Dad, what is going on with you, what were you doing so late last night and how did you lose the last few weeks?" Bas insisted as he raised a small window in the kitchen to let in some fresh air and the noise of the city.

"I was watching a documentary series on the cold war and having a scotch…or two… and I was…uh…binging. You know, like Netflix and chill, for me it was the history channel and scotch." Paul flashed a half grin and raised his eyebrows.

"No, Dad, no… that is not the same thing." Bas laughed at Paul's 'dad joke' and sat down at the kitchen island, watching his dad finish the scrambled eggs and spread some butter on the toasted bread. Bas wasn't even hungry, but the smell of the toasted bread suddenly had him salivating. His dad's eggs were always perfectly cooked, perfectly seasoned and perfectly cheesy. Paul plated up breakfast and with steam rising from the eggs, slid them across the counter to Bas and the empty chair. Paul shuffled around the broad island and joined his son. The two began to eat without saying anything more.

"It has been three weeks since you were here last, huh? I guess I may have fallen in a hole a bit more than usual." Paul broke the silence with his question.

Bas was glad that his dad could admit it. It would make his next request much easier, "So Dad, I planned to stay a few extra days this trip. I thought maybe you and I could go up to Morris Cove, stay at the beach house for a couple days.

What do you think, will it work for you?"

Paul looked up from his eggs and stared across the room blankly. He felt like there was an ulterior motive there somewhere. He couldn't quite place it yet; it sounded so innocent. And he literally had nothing going on for the next few days except another docuseries on the potential impacts of a viral apocalypse on the world. "Sure, Bas, we can go up. It will be a little chilly this time of year, but the views are good. What did you have in mind we'd do there? Netflix and —"

"I'm gonna stop you right there, Dad." Bas put his hand up jokingly and turned to his dad. "Dad, you haven't done anything new since Mom passed."

"What do you mean, I just told you about that cold war documentary! That is new, your mom never liked binging shows, a waste of time to her." Paul snapped back, with a smile.

"You know what I mean, Dad," Bas put down his fork, closed his eyes and pinched the bridge of his nose. "You haven't seen any friends. You have been hiding away lately. Have you painted or done any drawings? Anything?"

Art has always been Paul's creative outlet. It's where his emotions were set free and he could find his voice, his expression. Bas was right, since Peg was lost, he hadn't picked up a brush, pencil...nothing. Not even a doodle. He lost his passion when he lost her. Peg was the thing that grounded him, helped him sort through the clutter in his mind. Now, there was too much. Too much to think about and at the same time, not enough to think about. Everything in his life went dark when he lost her. He thought he was strong, and he learned that she made him strong. The best parts of him were cultivated by her; she fed him and made him grow. Peg challenged Paul in ways that no one else he knew did. She was able to help him see new perspectives and discover his own feelings about issues, society, people, relationships. She was his biggest fan and his most delicate critic. She always told him the truth and she did it in a way that he could hear it and was never hurt by it. Peg made him a better person and what had he become now that she was gone?

"Dad?" Bas interrupted Paul's internal monologue. "Are you ok?" Bas could see emptiness in his dad's eyes. Bas had to get him to agree go away to the beach house with him. If he could just get him out of this apartment, maybe that would help bring him back. After a few more minutes of convincing, Bas was successful and his dad agreed to go away with him. They both needed a change in scenery, Bas had been busier than normal for the year and this break was going to be good for both of them. He didn't even know what he could do or should do for his dad, he just knew he didn't want to lose him too.

Paul carefully folded a few shirts and two pairs of jeans and packed them in his Weekender bag. Packing for this trip became a meticulous task, but he wasn't sure why. Pajamas, underwear, socks, sweats, running shoes…just in case… and toothbrush, toothpaste, moisturizer, shaving cream, razor… what else… medication…check, check, check. Paul took another look and did a mental rundown of the contents of his bag. Was he stalling? Why would he waste time, what is stopping him? Spending time with his kids and especially Bas was a highlight for Paul; Bas was his "mini-me." It wasn't Bas, it was Paul. Paul knew that if he took this trip, it would be a turning point for him. Either he would succumb to his darker thoughts, or he would come out of the fog of grief and start to live again. He knew these were the decisions before him, but even knowing the weight, he struggled with the choice. It had been two years since Peg was taken and she was still able to talk him into leaving the house and getting a new perspective. This trip was going to be a journey through him — a discovery of himself — and he had to be brave for her sake, to push himself through it.

Bas took Paul's bag, and both stepped out the door into the hallway. First step, Paul thought, this is the first step somewhere. He turned and locked the door, then met Bas at the elevator.

"Here we go," Paul sighed as he stepped in and Bas pushed the button for the lobby.

The drive was a little less than two hours from New York to New Haven, Connecticut. The clean, salty air was a welcome change from the stench of the city. No matter where you live in New York, you can't escape the odor of car exhaust, sewer steam and hot dog carts. Peg and Paul had inherited the little house off Townshend Street that overlooks Morris Cove, from Peg's Uncle Oscar. He had no children and was only married briefly before he agreed with his ex that he was a confirmed bachelor and gave her most of their conjugal property, including cars and their home upstate, but he kept the house in New Haven. Oscar stayed there until he passed away from lymphoma seventeen years ago. It wasn't grandiose, it was three small bedrooms, a nice, big family room, smaller kitchen and only one bathroom, but it was a comfortable, peaceful place. Peg was happy to keep this part of Oscar just the way it was. They were always close when she was growing up and she loved seeing the old family pictures over the piano in the front room. It was a piece of her history frozen in time. When Oscar passed and handed down the place to Peg, she didn't want to change a thing. It took some time before she made it her own, trading out the seventies style furniture for coastal patterns and bohemian styles. She kept the pictures - new frames - but kept the pictures. Some things shouldn't be forgotten so fast.

Peg still had more renovations in mind to add on space for the grandkids to stay and a swing set in the back. She was doing some shopping in the city that day; picking up some ornaments for her garden – she had found these perfect stones shaped like herbs. She was shopping for a small greenhouse that she could take to the beach house and grow seedlings there before moving them to her main garden. She was looking up; the clouds were wispy and the sky was such a bright and vibrant blue. The air was crisp and there were pigeons cooing in the eave of the building behind her. The medical examiner said that he couldn't quite determine if she'd had the heart attack before the car hit her or after. Everything happened so fast, it was hard to tell which came first. Peg was always healthy, and Paul wanted to believe so badly that if that car hadn't run the light, he'd still have her. Maybe there was a reason she was looking up and didn't see the car coming. Maybe Peg knew what was next and the last thing she could do was look up and see the beauty of the world before she moved on.

Paul and Bas made some small talk as they carried the bags inside. It was almost dinner time now and they needed to figure out if they would try to get a few groceries in town or call for a pizza. Weariness prevailed and a pizza for dinner won the flip. The pizza was lukewarm by the time the delivery driver made it to the house. The two sat at the round cafe table in the kitchen eating from the box and having a few laughs over some leftover IPAs in the fridge. They caught up on the last three weeks, mostly news from Bas and his wife. A lonely slice of pepperoni was still in the box surrounded by a few beer bottles. It was nearly 8pm and there was a sliver of orange, purple and red sitting just above the ocean horizon. Paul and Bas took the party to the wrap-around porch in the front that faced the ocean and sat in the wooden rockers silently as they watched that sliver of color slowly disappear. The patch of beach where their house set was a mix of sandy spots and large rocks extending to the grassy areas of the coast. The waves crashed hard against the rocks but the sound was oddly smooth and tranquil. Paul hadn't been at the beach house since Peg died. He tried to mask the strange feeling he had being there without her and hoped Bas wouldn't pick up on it. Everything was empty, or maybe just that everything was a little less. Days were a little less bright, nights were a little less restful and the only thing that he felt more of was loneliness.

"I think I have had enough for today, Dad," Bas said, "I am going to call Anna and turn in. Will you be okay out here?" Paul scoffed at his question, "I'll be just fine son," and he looked up at him with his best dad face, that look dads give when their teenager has just dissed classic rock, "Go on and tell that girl of yours her almost father-in-law says hi and good night." Both men smiled, barely, and Bas opened the wooden screen door to head in for bed.

Bas knew that his dad would be fighting some demons this weekend, but he couldn't watch him deteriorate like this any longer. Paul needed to fight this himself and Bas knew that too. The best he could do for his dad is to make sure he had meals, took a shower and got some sunshine. There was no need for Bas to force a lecture or a discussion, he just intended to be quiet and be around if his dad needed him.

Alone on the porch, Paul could see the lights near the beach flicker on as dusk settled in against the sand and grass and rock. The darkness settled in him too. He really felt it now, the loss of her, as he stared at the empty chair beside him. Bas startled him a bit when he came back to the door, "Dad, are you ready to go to bed?" It had been almost an hour and half; Bas had talked with Anna, showered and checked a few work emails before coming to the door to lock up.

Paul's eyes widened as he looked up at his son, blinking slowly. Bas was just as surprised to see Paul still in the same place he left him as Paul was to see Bas. Paul lost time again. Where did he go, and how long should Bas let him disappear before getting him some real help.

Might as well go to bed, Paul thought, he was still feeling the effects of the scotch he'd had for dinner the night before and he was ready to get in bed and start over. Start all the way over, and maybe he would be able to find a way to save her.

The morning light didn't pierce his eyes so harshly here as it did in the city. Paul stretched slowly and turned on his side away from the window. He was on her side of the bed now. The crystal and gold bracelet caught the rays peeking through the drapes and cast a prism on the wall. She must have left it here the last time. There was so much of her in this place, maybe that is why he had stayed away. The distressed, wood of the bed frame and floral bedding; the lounger that sat at the end of the bed was an estate sale 'find' that Peg restored and recovered in complementing fabric. On the walls of the master bedroom, she had pictures of their kids at varying ages and in different sizes, protected by antique frames she had picked up here and there. Paul wiped his eyes with both hands and let them fall heavily to his sides as he looked up to the ceiling. He could almost see her face through the foggy mist of his droopy eyes, he could almost take in her signature lavender scent in the room. Paul blinked again and she was gone.

The kitchen was quiet, and it was pretty early, considering Paul's usual routine. Bas left a note on the table that he had gone running and then planned to go into town for some essentials and snacks and he would be back to make breakfast. "He is always taking care of me," Paul thought with a twinge of sarcasm. He was far too young to be fussed over like that. Although lately, the beach house was only used on occasion by the kids, there were a few staples still in the cupboard and Paul found a box of instant coffee packets and emptied the contents of a packet into a cup. He rummaged through the cabinets for a small pot and started boiling water for his coffee.

Peg walked through the kitchen to the stove where the water sat bubbling. Paul's eyes widened as she grabbed the handle, "Now Paul," she said, "this instant coffee is just no good, filled with nastiness. Why don't you have some proper beans here to throw in the grinder?" Peg continued fiddling with the pot on the stove. "Aw Peg, you know I am no snob, I don't mind the instant stuff. It gets the job done." Paul was comfortable now in the ruse, and he nestled behind her as she stood at the stove. "After all these years you still don't mind taking care of me," he whispered in the back of her ear. Peg turned her head over her shoulder and smiled at Paul, then got back to pouring the hot water over the instant crystals sending the aroma through the kitchen. Paul's eyes closed slightly as he smelled the coffee and felt the warmth of Peg close to him.

"Dad?" Bas was in the doorway of the kitchen holding grocery bags, scrunching his nose to identify the smell of the burnt pan. He quickly dropped them on the table and made his way to the stove, nudged his dad aside and turned off the burner under the pot, that was now boiled dry and burning.

Peg faded away into the steam that had billowed from the pot. Paul snapped back and found Bas cleaning up his burnt mess. It had happened again. Twice now since they arrived at the beach house. If he was honest with himself, it was happening more and more lately that he found himself in his memory rather than in his reality. And if he were even more honest – he felt more peace in his memory.

There was no way that he could keep this up. Paul knew that he wasn't fooling his kids and it wouldn't be too long before they "took action," whatever that action might be. He also knew that he was not made for nursing homes. He was still a healthy guy, kind of; he ate a couple of times a day and got some exercise. Although his mind seemed to race more than anything else. Paul felt strong and vibrant when he was in his mind, his memory. The real world felt pale and gray, like an echo of a dream. But when he would close his eyes at night – or even in the day just for a second to remember – the sun gave hues of daisies and marigolds and hyacinths. The sky was as blue as the sapphire of her eyes and the air around him was crisp and it smelled like her.

Bas met Paul on the porch where he was already in his rocker staring straight out with sullen eyes. Bas could see the embarrassment on his dad's face and he didn't think it was a good time to get into what just happened. But at some point, he had to address it. What if his dad had been alone? He could have burned his apartment down, could have hurt somebody or hurt himself. Bas wondered how long this "spacing out" has been going on. How many close calls had there been? How many more close calls will there be?

Bas took the seat next to Paul and matched his mood. He kept his gaze straight and waited for his dad to speak. Bas waited for what felt like forever.

"It's just been so different, ya know," Paul could barely say the words. "At home... I look out in the greenhouse and I am always surprised I don't see her. When I wake up in the morning, and I am alone, I forget she is gone and I expect she is in the kitchen messing around or that she just went to the market," it was flowing out of him now and Paul felt more at ease talking about it with Bas. "It is something I have held onto since she left, I just couldn't or didn't want to let you in on it. Sometimes, in my mind, I can see her, Bas. Not like a dream, like she is here, now and more real to me than you are sometimes. I don't know when it will happen... when I lose myself. It's like I will catch a scent, something that reminds me of her. When I was making the coffee, that instant coffee and the strong smell of it immediately took me back to a time when your mother scolded me for using that freeze dried, no patience, instant stuff." Paul was grinning a bit now thinking of it. "I could see her Bas, she was right there in the kitchen, scolding me again. I know it was her...but not her... like an echo of her. But Bas, I would trade an echo of her for sitting here on a clear day looking out into the beauty of that sea rolling in or the green leaves in the garden on the roof that she spent so much time or almost anything... I would trade anything to have her again even for a second."

Bas was overwhelmed at his father's confession. He knew that his mom's death had been hard on Paul. He just thought that with his sisters and all their families around that his dad would come out of that fog he was trapped in just after it happened. A new reality was setting in for Bas. His dad had been putting on a mask, a happy face when they were all together, well, that new reality was like a punch in the gut to him. Bas couldn't understand how his dad would rather be in that make-believe memory than present with him, or June or Minnie. His sisters had a lot going on with their own families and their jobs and... Bas was starting to see it now. It is by no fault of theirs, it is just the way life works. Kids grow up, get married, have careers, move away, come back – but it is never the same as when everyone was home; when everyone called home the same home. They didn't neglect Paul, or ignore him. But day in and day out, real or memory, Peg was there with Paul. When the kids couldn't make it to dinner on a Sunday, Paul had take-out and watched silly movies with Peg's echo next to him on the sofa. When there was snow two feet high last winter and no one could get out of their doors, Paul heated up soup from a can while sitting under a blanket, talking about the days he and Peg would take walks through Central Park in the summer. Peg was always the one Paul painted. In canvas and in life, she was his inspiration. He lost his person.

"I love you, Dad," Bas told Paul with a strong voice, without wavering, even though he was crumbling after seeing these wilted pieces of his dad. Bas knew that he had to talk to his sisters, he knew that his dad was going to come to a fork in the road soon.

The two just sat in near silence for the next couple of hours. There was a faint sound of people, kids playing on the beach. The less noise they made sitting on that porch, the louder the noise around them became. The sun was getting lower. They both seemed lost in thought until Bas cut through the quiet. "Hey Dad, how about we go into town and get a pizza and a little fresh air?" Paul's eyes widened a bit, he turned toward Bas and gave him a grin. "Maybe we stop at that bar and have a beer and play a little eight-ball?' Bas returned a smile, "I think we can manage that." Bas stood up and stretched and Paul did the same. They both did an up and down look at each other and decided their attire was good enough for the local pub, so they grabbed their keys and phones and wallets from the entry table, locked the door and jumped in the car.

Paul's face was brighter, he'd had a good day and it was about to get better he thought. He and his boy, out on the town. Well, out on the small town, but a town, nonetheless. Bas was excited too, Paul could see it on his face. Bas parked the car and they trucked into the pub, and grabbed a table near a pool table with a less common, red felt that may have seen better days. An outgoing, ponytailed, woman in her forties sidled up to the table with a couple of menus and told them all about the specials. The "boys" gave her their order and settled in for a while. They talked and laughed telling stories about high school and college; about Minnie's latest thrift outing with her twins and how much they run her and her wife around. They were only two and they had clear opinions even though they could barely talk enough to tell what they were. Paul and Bas played some pool and had a couple of beers and just enjoyed each other and enjoyed "the now." Bas thought maybe his dad was turning that corner. This trip was good for them. It was good to have the time together and it was good to get his dad out of his head. In fact, they were having such a good time that they barely noticed the time. It was getting late. Bas said it first, that they better start heading out. He only had two beers with dinner; let his dad have all the fun and stay well enough to drive home.

Pulling into the drive at the beach house this late was so familiar. Paul remembered this many times, hauling the kids in while they slept, Peg lugging all their stuff. He could see the way the light from the moon was hitting her face just right and made it glow. When she smiled back at him it was like the stars just came down and settled in her eyes. Paul blinked. Bas was looking at him and they were both still in the car in the drive. Bas's face was gentle as he watched his dad's eyes turn gray again. "Are you ready to go in, Dad?" He knew that Paul had come back. In the short time, observing his dad he noticed that his eyes changed when he came back.

Bas poured himself a night cap from the bar cart in the living room. The whiskey had been there awhile but it was still good. Paul wanted a small one as well. In the family room, there was a table with a chess board constructed into the wood of the table. It was set up with pieces and ready to go. "How about a game," Paul asked Bas. Paul taught him how to play when he was young, on that table in fact. Again, they had some laughs, played their game and had their whiskey.

"I may have taught you too well," Paul said, "Are we at a stalemate here?"

"Nah, I think I can take you, but let's finish it in the morning. We will both be thinking clearer then," Bas winked and tipped his glass toward his dad before taking the last gulp and standing up to go to bed. Paul responded with his glass and they said good night. Bas finished up in the bathroom and stopped in the hall when he saw his dad moving the pillows off the bed before climbing into it. "I had a real good day, Dad. I love you, good night."

"I love you too, son. It was a great day." Paul had a peaceful face, he went to Bas and gave him a hard hug. Bas went to his room and called Anna. It was late there, but not too bad. He told her about the day, what his dad said about his gaps, how they had such a good time and he thought things may be looking up and his dad may be coming out of that fog. Anna was always there to support him, this was no different. They said their good nights and Bas went to sleep.

The morning came too early today, or maybe the night ended too late. The light from the sun came in through the slats in the blinds and one ray in particular was burning a hole in his forehead like it was shining through a magnifying glass on an anthill. Bas rolled over to escape it. He opened his eyes slowly and stretched. He smiled again thinking about the game of pool last night. He won twenty bucks off his dad when he made that last shot of eight-ball. The money was no big deal, but the win was nice... Bas liked to win with his dad; showed his dad that he was a good student lapping up all the knowledge he could from him. That reminded him of their chess game, surely Paul was up by now and they could finish it. Bas took a little time and freshened up in the bathroom and went to the kitchen to start some coffee, laid out some bacon and eggs too. He would make some breakfast before they finished their game.

"Dad...hey ...Dad, are you up yet?" Bas rounded the corner of the hall to his dad's room and saw him still in bed sleeping. "Too much sauce last night, huh? You aren't as young as you used to be, Dad." Paul didn't answer, and he didn't move. Bas's heart started beating a little harder, and his palms were getting sweaty. He stepped in the room and closer to the bed. His mouth was dry now as he reached over and touched his dad's shoulder. Bas knew straightaway. He pulled the blankets up and quietly walked out of the room and closed the door. Once on the other side, he instantly felt hot tears run down his cheeks.

He called Anna, then his sisters and then the police. He didn't quite know the order of things but that felt right. They would be there by evening. The police and coroner came in less than an hour. Bas was on the porch in his dad's rocker when they arrived. There would be an autopsy, by Bas's request, and they would know more after that. Bas was still, quietly answered all their questions and took his seat on the porch again when they pulled away. It all changed in a moment.

Evening came and the house was full. Minnie's kids were playing and watching cartoons on cable, and the siblings decided to talk a little bit about what was next. Bas couldn't hold back anymore. "June, you know he said he saw Mom. All the time, he could see her and said that she was more real to him than you or me. He had...spells, gaps... where I could see he wasn't there anymore or at least he wasn't here. He was lost in his mind. He almost burned down the kitchen trying to heat water up for coffee," Bas knew what he was saying was probably coming as a surprise to his sisters. "Then last night, we had such a great, great night. It was like old times, we were laughing and cutting up, telling stories and playing games. It was like before Mom died. I thought we were getting him back…"

Bas's cell phone rang and broke the conversation. It was an unknown local number, so he went to the porch to take the call.

"Takotsubo Cardiomyopathy. That is what the coroner said," Bas came through the screen door as he was talking to his sisters. "There was no other signs of blockages that could have caused a heart attack but the shape of his heart suggested it was this… Takotsu - "

"Broken heart syndrome," Anna said quietly and moved to stand by Basil. There was a stillness in the room that couldn't be explained. One of the twins pointed toward the kitchen and smiled. They might be gone but Paul and Peg wouldn't be forgotten. Not in this place and not with these people that loved them.

Paul climbed in to bed and got situated on his side of the bed, with the blankets pulled up close. For a second he could smell flowers, was it Peg's perfume, maybe so. Paul closed his eyes and he was sitting at the table in their garden on the roof of their apartment building. Peg was across from him. He smiled at her widely and told her all about the night he'd had. He reached for her and she gave him her hand. For the first time, since Paul started seeing her, he could finally touch her. Peg's hand was warm in his and he held it tight, then took it with both hands. He was crying just a little. Somewhere he understood the choice he was making. He always knew he would make that trade. His muse. Hand in hand, admiring the beautiful flowers around them, the sun set between the buildings.

TWO HEARTS

She has a lonely heart, an old soul
She was little more than a girl
When She first knew love.
Then that love – Her greatest love – was lost.

Pompous brilliance, not yet a man
As He came to her. The two shared life and
hope.
Hope with plans to make, promises to keep
But life was too long and love too short.
Faith in vain for the return of Him

She dreams of what it could be now
If only that love would be restored.
She hopes in vain for the one that keeps Her heart;
To return to the affection of their youth.

Love tempts and mocks Her tender but critical
heart.
All who dare to approach Her, fall shy of Her
measure.
Her timid, broken soul cannot risk
The chore of losing again.

She believes He lives a lie, denying His heart.
Conceit, guilt, shame are his rewards.

A game of two hearts
joined and torn apart:
She waits. He lives.
Both wonder.

LUCKY NUMBER SEVENS

She stood on the corner of Washington and Fourth streets. It was not yet night and still, the dusky, winter chill allowed her to see the silver stream of breath as she exhaled when she slid her gloves on. Night was the hardest. She was leaving work later than she planned today. She hiked her laptop bag further on her shoulder and juggled her purse as she felt it slip down to her forearm. It was a short walk from her office to the parking lot. But in those short minutes between sundown and darkness, the two blocks turned into two miles. A man, in crumpled clothes with a smudge of dirt under his right eye and again near the left corner of his mouth, held his half-gloved hand up to her. No words, just looking up at her from his hunched stature. She could almost taste the stench of Wild Turkey. She learned by now – don't make eye contact; walk fast, with a purpose – yet he had surprised her tonight. She reached quickly to her coat pocket for the leftover change from her vending machine jaunt earlier in the afternoon. No time for lunch today, she took a 15-minute smoke break and chowed on some plain potato chips and went back to work. The change couldn't have totaled more than forty-five cents, but it was enough to satisfy the man. He looked in his hand, straightened his stocking hat and pocketed the coins. He gave a slight nod and turned from her to stumble off in the opposite direction, muttering something incoherent under his breath. He stood there every night when she went past. Most nights she got lucky, some nights he did.

She rarely noticed his features before, only his beat-up clothes, the holes in his hat, the dirt on his fingertips and the bourbon on his breath. Tonight, she detected a softness in his eyes. She wondered how he came to be the man he is. What had he been before? Would he ever be anything else? Maybe there was some tragedy in his family... Maybe he lost his wife. Maybe he lost a child... what must you lose to lead you to lose it all. How many years had she walked by him and never thought of this? She probably gave him less than fifty dollars in a year, but shouldn't this exchange warrant that she learns a little about him? This grimy, disheveled man was a staple in her life, in her routine and she knew nothing but speculation about him.

She found her car, pressed the key-fob and heard the driver's door unlock. She threw her bag and purse on the floor of the passenger side, glided to the seat and locked the door. Her actions were routine. Get up, go to work, have meetings, interact, pack up, go to the car. These were static, unchanged. Here she could pretend nothing is different. Here she could be the same.

Once she sat behind the wheel, she began to disintegrate. Two different people – both share the same face. Responsibility always won out with

her. Do the job; find the solution; make it work –
these were her mantras. Why not now? She
turned the key and slowly shifted into gear. She
was the oldest child in her family; she was no
stranger to duty and obligation. Her parents relied
on her for help with the house, help with her
siblings. She was smart, very smart, and applied
herself to get scholarships and work-study
programs to fund her college education. She had
never wanted to be a burden on her parents. She
took control of her future and felt responsible for
its success or failure. Failure. Is that what is
happening?

Her eyes refocused on the white and yellow
lines against the asphalt ahead of her. Traffic was
unusually light tonight. Seven minutes to the
highway, thirty-seven minutes to the exit,
seventeen minutes to the driveway. Make this
routine so her thoughts don't have a chance to
surface again. Is that even possible? It must be.
What is the price of pushing down a feeling so
deep, that it fades into something fuzzy and nearly
forgotten – like a dream that looks like a movie, or
a memory made of stories and pictures but no
experience. But no, she can't think about that
now, the exit is coming up.

The garage door is already open when she
pulls in the driveway and the door to the house is
unlocked; he is already home. The television is
loud, as she opens the door and steps inside. He
sits on the couch in the living room, and she can

see him visibly tense as she walks closer to the couch. She manages to shift her head toward him to say hello; he doesn't look at her but returns the greeting with an upward nod. To her right, she sees the crumpled take-out bags from the fast-food taco place cluttered on the kitchen table. Just as well he already ate, she isn't hungry despite the snack size bag of chips that served as her lunch. From the corner of her eye, she sees unmade boxes leaning against the piano bench in the front room and quietly sighs to herself. His hand rests steadily on the cable remote, his gaze un-shifted as she makes her way across the living room, careful not to obstruct his view or draw his attention. She stops for a moment, behind the sofa and looks widely at the scene before her, then lowers her eyes and turns toward the stairs.

It is almost seven and almost the seventh. Nothing more she can pack, might as well go to sleep.

THE GLOW

A girl stood silent in a grassy grove and all of a
sudden a glow began to grow
It was warm and bright across the meadow.

She ran and ran to it as fast as she could,
But she only found herself deeper and deeper into
the wood.

She could feel it expanding; she could see it clear;
It seemed so far from her, yet she felt it so near.

The girl thought she might catch it, hold it in her
hand,
But the closer she came, it slipped through her
fingers like sand.

It had the most brilliant effects, deep golden
shimmer, an exquisite find;
She knew it was a genuine one of a kind.

When she got close enough she felt the light cool
on her face but warm inside,
But she just couldn't catch it, no matter how hard
she tried.

Her body was tired, her mind confused,
Her soul was weakened, her ego bruised.

She slumped, kind of slowly, in a soft pile to the

ground
Arms limp, palms upward, against a tree mound.

Then a little man appeared, as if out of thin air
His kind eyes brought the girl out of despair.

*"My dear," he said gently, "What has made you so
troubled?"*

*"The light, sir, can't you see it?" she quietly said. "I
see it everywhere, all around me. It's lovely and bright.
It touches everything I can see, although I can't touch
it. It reaches every inch of the meadow, yet I can't
reach it. I want it so badly, but how do I catch it?"*

Her sad eyes returned their gaze to the tall grass,
green and swaying from the breeze.

His voice was strong as he took her hands softly
and lifted her gently from her knees.

*"You can't catch the light. The light catches you. Don't
run anymore. Stay still. It has always been in you. You
have only just now noticed what we have seen all along."*

THE GOLDEN SWORD

There once was a beautiful princess that lived in a splendid land with high mountains and crystal-clear streams. There were bright green meadows and rich dark woods...but the land was also riddled with skirmishes and wars because the people grew selfish and greedy and wanted more and more power.

When she was young, she loved to roam the land and swim in the streams and lay in the bright green grass and let the blades tickle her ears as her ebony hair fanned around her face and the sun kissed her porcelain skin. She longed for those carefree days. Now she must stay inside the castle's thick, rock walls to keep her safe; to keep her protected; to keep her isolated. Every day, she went to the King and pleaded with him to let her be free again to see the land she loved so much. Every day, the King denied her plea... until...

A strange visitor, a peddler, came to the palace from a nearby kingdom. He requested an audience with the King to tell him about his wares and how well they would fare in his kingdom. The King was wary of this visitor and his claims; however, he granted the peddler's request. As he was showing the King his silver and weaponry, the princess came into the court with her daily plea for a stroll through the land. Grateful for the distraction of his daughter, the King welcomed her into his throne room and the visitor looked down and away from the beauty of the girl, out of respect for his host. The King, once again, heard his princess ask for the freedom to roam the lands again, to feel the sand of the streams between her toes and the sun shining full on her face. The visitor could no longer keep quiet, he spoke up to the King softly and told him he had just the thing for the girl, to keep her safe; to keep her protected. He drew from his bag a glimmering, golden sword. It was enormous to the girl, almost the size of her. The peddler said that if she carried this with her as she strode through the country, no war would harm her; no person could touch her. The princess, knowing what a hardship it would be to carry such a burden, gladly accepted the sword and promised her King that she would be safe, and protected; he needn't worry. So, the King agreed but insisted the peddler remain in his castle until his daughter's return.

So, the princess took the sword and set off through the court and to the gates of the castle. Admittedly, she grew weary from the golden beast just making it past the gates, but she knew that once she was in the breeze of the meadows and the warmth of the sun, the heaviness would feel as light as a feather. So, she walked on, through the gates, over the bridge and into the kingdom.

But what she saw around her brought her instant sadness. The wars and fighting had scarred the land she loved. The plush green meadows were brown and the blades of grass that playfully tickled her toes were now hard and brittle and poked her ankles like needles as she made her way through them. The clouds in the sky hid the yellow sun from her and she pulled her cloak around her shoulders to fight a chill. The streams were dirty from the men drenching themselves with its clear water after days of battle. The princess grew more and more saddened by each step she took through this darkened land. Each step, her heart grew as heavy as the sword she tugged behind her. She saw the streets of their village scorched by fire and her people cold, tired and hungry. She knew she could find the green grasses again, drink from the clear waters and feel the heat from the sky again. So, she kept walking. Her golden protection trailing behind, slowing her steps, her breath heavy. She walked and walked to the borders of the kingdom, over every step of the land that was now unrecognizable to her. She went on, through the mountains and the valleys and she grew tired. Her pace was so slow, and she could barely lift the golden sword. The peddler was right, no harm came to her while she wielded or rather, pulled the golden hunk behind her. No physical harm, anyway. Her heart ached for the people of her kingdom and for where they had allowed themselves to sink…far into the depths of despair, loneliness, selfishness, pride and pity. She knew them as different people. She knew them happy, smiling, and bright.

The princess had to stop. Darkness was falling. She couldn't make her trek anymore. She had to sleep. She thought, maybe, if she slept, she would awaken to a new world around her, where the sun shone, and she wasn't cold or tired or laden with such a burden in her heart and in her hands. So tired… so weary… so sad… so lonely. So, she slept.

The girl dreamt of the land she played in as a girl. Of the people laughing and the streets full of children and full of life. Night passed and the morning brought a sliver of sun, through a sky of orange and purple and blue. The princess opened her big, dark eyes and for a second, felt the familiar warmth. For a second the grass beneath her felt softer, the breeze smelled sweeter. She awoke with hope. Hope because today, she knew she had found something of what she knew before. Inspired by this, the princess found new strength to carry the sword up high, out in front of her, through the streets of the town again. As she did, the people in the streets looked up. They saw the tiny princess hoisting the heavy sword over her shoulder. Something about her made them stop what they were doing and watch. She was worn out, her hair disheveled, her dress in ribbons at the hem from her journey, but her face was bright, and her eyes were smiling. She was strong, although she looked weak. They saw the determination in her, the love, the strength and the hope. With that single act, she changed the people. She changed her land.

As the princess passed back through the castle gates, her father, the King stood, arms open waiting for her. He was a kind and loving man and was distraught that his lovely daughter was in the cold and brutal kingdom alone. He scooped up his girl and held her with all the love he had in his heart. He too, saw the difference in her...and then he saw the people.

Following the princess, quietly and reverently were the people of the village. Unknowingly, the princess had led them back to the castle and beyond the gates, before the bridge they stood, then they knelt...curtsied, fell to their faces in humility, in shame, begging the King's forgiveness for the destruction they wrought upon his land. The King turned again to his daughter; his eyes wet with happiness. He took the golden sword from her and held it high above his head. The princess did what no one else had been able to do. She carried the burden of the King, of the people and came out stronger than when she left. The sword hung on the palace walls to remind all the people of the sacrifice, the journey and the love of a land and a life that would never be forgotten.

HEAT

Heat trickled slow down both sides of her face.
Her look remained stone; no one would know,
But for the wetness on her cheeks, how she was
breaking.
From a distance, her smile was stoic, her eyes
were steel.
Closer, the corners of her mouth were pasted to
her dimples,
Her lids were held open with invisible toothpicks.
She wanted to curl up, like a baseball in a glove,
wrapping the leather around her to hide.
She turned to the side, patted her cheeks and
pinched them for color.
Her dress was beautiful, her hair in place,
make-up, still impeccable.

Facade of splendor.

PEOPLE WILL FALL

People will fall, creep, slither or rise into a few categories. The way people in these categories interact with one another is based on my own experience and interpretation of those I have witnessed to be in these groups. I love everyone that is in my circle, and don't go trying to figure out what category I am in because even I don't know that yet. Most people probably oscillate between all of them. Now, the definition of these categories may get a little messy – so hold on tight, here we go.

To start, we have the "FIRSTS" who can be defined by their great childhood. And I mean truly great, some may even call them spoiled. "FIRSTS" usually peaked in high school. They had cool clothes, latest styles and all the popular gadgets. Hair doodads and video games, all of the hottest stuff, they had it. The other kids always crowded around them to see what they were doing. When they played sports, all the other kids cheered for them – every time. Theirs was the house that everyone wanted to be on prom night for the after party. Their parents either wanted to give them everything they didn't have or wanted to keep the status quo and continue the tradition of making childhood great. Now, once these "FIRSTS" have grown to adulthood, they find themselves always trying to get back to those glory days, when they had it all. Back to a time when their needs were taken care of and no one came to them for answers – well, not real answers anyway. "FIRSTS" need to be in the center of it, whether it's a conversation or an activity. Sometimes this has been described as self-involved, egotistical – narcissistic.

Inevitably, "FIRSTS" go looking to recapture this feeling of youthful euphoria and a carefree life in their partners. The "FIRSTS" are drawn to people that replace that parental comfort, leaving them to concern themselves with less important things than house payments and college tuition. "FIRSTS" are put in charge of things like picking a restaurant or the color of the new car. This is absolutely not to say that "FIRSTS" are bad people. Just young people. Imagine for a second that reincarnation is real. "FIRSTS" would be new – where this time around is their first time around.

Now we have the "NEXTS," and they are really interesting. "NEXTS" had some bumps in the road growing up. They liked high school but were ready to get on with life halfway through sophomore year. "NEXTS" always liked responsibility, having the answers, being someone that others could depend on and (you guessed it) having someone to take care of someday. Usually, these are the eldest children, feeling that need to be responsible and sometimes birth order has nothing to do with it. "NEXTS" want to please people, not in an insecure way, but in a way that lets the other person know they are thinking about them and want their happiness. As adults, "NEXTS" are hardworking, and usually rise slowly. They don't toot their own horn, they wait for someone to notice all the great work they do and reward them for it. They prefer to be behind the scenes, making others look good and smiling to themselves knowing that without their help their boss would have flopped that presentation. But again, those smiles aren't snickers – they do those things because they care about the people that they do them for and want them to succeed. And, this categorization of "NEXTS" is usually a temporary one – just a stepping stone through the shallow river of life.

It isn't an outlandish assumption that the "FIRSTS" and the "NEXTS" very often find each other. These relationships can last a lifetime. Both types of people get exactly what they need. One loving their life on a pedestal and the other loving that they can be the one to give that life. It is like they fit together like a puzzle. But let's be realistic, over half of marriages end in a split and we can't even count the number of non-legally binding relationships that end, so if these puzzle pieces fit so perfectly, what is happening?

Here is a theory: The "NEXTS" in those relationships sometimes figure out that maybe their whole life doesn't have to be about pleasing someone that can be pleased exclusively by a time machine. Now that they know this, what can they do? The "FIRSTS" need to be taken care of and will just go on demanding their way, because it gives them some control over an adult life that they didn't want. So for the "NEXTS" that have made this life-altering realization that there may be something more that they have to offer and something more that they want from life, they start a metamorphosis to a new category… "LASTS."

The name of this new classification is mostly because this is it for them. These "LASTS" will have to overcome the binds of duty and responsibility to change their life that their past choices defined for them. Or they will accept the failure and retreat from a level of craziness they can never fix, destined to remain in the position of maintaining the pedestal. So, in order to survive, or in order to make it to the next level, they delve into a domain of self-improvement. Or, more aptly described as self-exploration.

"LASTS" need to find the answer to the question of why they are here, what is their purpose, how they can add something to the world and also why they stay in a relationship that isn't feeding them…even though they know the answer will separate them from their "FIRSTS" partners even further. "FIRSTS" can't follow a path that looks deeper in themselves because they are afraid of what they may find. When people make that decision to look internally, there is an unspoken commitment to acknowledge what is there, and admit it, even if it isn't great. And then the hardest part: do something about the nasty bits.

So, the "LASTS" continue their sabbaticals into the depths of their soul, improving and growing alone. Misery in silence until a choice is presented that will seal their fate, one way or another.

Now, what if two "NEXTS" were to meet just as they begin their soulful journey to find out who they are and who they want to be? Neither is chained to the victories of the past and the present is just a result of the decisions made to affect the future. That world is open to all possibilities.

But...remember who the "NEXTS" are and who they were originally drawn to – that is right... "FIRSTS." And "FIRSTS" are friendly with other "FIRSTS" reliving the old days, playing a game of one-ups and polishing their feigning crowns together. This means the meeting of these two "NEXTS" is usually a product of a friendship of their respective "FIRSTS." The world full of potential will never come to be, because neither "NEXT" will rid themselves of the chains of their "FIRSTS."

So, let's recap. We have "FIRSTS" that will never change. They may look like they change, but the reality is the programming of their brain prevents real change. To their death bed, they cannot overcome themselves...ever. There are the "FIRSTS" that imprison their "NEXTS."

And we have "NEXTS" that will transform to "LASTS" but are never able to make the decision to move past it and will always remain in the power of their partners. They cannot help this any more than their partners cannot help not changing. Unavoidably, the "LASTS" will be stuck in this mindless cell where their thoughts are solely theirs and their creativity and growth can be seen by no one. There is no appreciation for their internal study, there is no reward, there is no happiness, there is survival.

This brings us to the final category, that I have not yet mentioned, and these are the best kind of people. They are the "ONLYS." These people are tricky. At first glance, they are mistaken for "NEXTS." But they never were. They know whomever they match, it doesn't matter, because they are not identified by that match. They know themselves already, even if they forget for a time. They were born knowing. They can do anything or nothing and it is always by their choice. They won't stay trapped in a mockery of life or be wasted coddling a partner that doesn't deserve it and they won't entertain someone who longs for and needs that partnership to satisfy the duty and responsibility that drives them.

"ONLYS" recognize their worth, even if they forget for a time. They can see the internal struggle and they battle it, learning about themselves and becoming better with each gratifying win and each devastating loss. Even when you think that they are weak and settling, they know they are strong and purposeful, even if they forget for a time. "ONLYS" love deeply, unconditionally, and forgive without reservation, because forgiveness is the thing that sets them free. They can be downtrodden and used, but they remember quickly who they are and who they will be, even if they forget for a time. "ONLYS" never give up.

Now, who are you?

If you are a "FIRST," you stopped reading long ago. Mostly because you identified with the content too closely and the revelation that your match will choose to be ultimately unhappy for your happiness has you in too much of a state to read further.

If you are a "NEXT," you are trying to figure out if you have realized the metamorphosis into the "LAST" and are wondering desperately how you can avoid that transparent prison that lies in wait for you...And that will keep you busy for some time.

And if you are an "ONLY," you have known forever these types of people described here. You have put all the people in your life in a category since the day you met them. You temper your relationships this way. Sometimes you have been fooled by your assumption of those you meet, because they resemble you so closely.

Sometimes you have been hurt by that assumption. But you know that you will get over it. You know that what you choose is always the best choice for you because you made it. You don't let people trade your life for theirs. There has always been a plan, a design for you. And there always will be…even if you forget for a time.

I was thinking that it might be a bonus to give you, as a reader, some context of my thought process as I wrote some of these stories and poems. I was going through some dark times, as I alluded in the foreword. Many of the poems are reflective of that, but I will recap a few of my favorites.

The Run is one of the greatest things I think I have written so far. I plan to expand it and Mile Marker 139 into a novel or novella at some point. And hey, if you are a critic and really hate it, keep it to yourself, I want to live in that bubble of fantasy. I like it because I feel like it addresses one of the most common questions we face as humans: whether or not to get involved in the tragedy of others' lives. And not just involved, but do we have the courage to act, stick up for someone you see being bullied, help out someone that is struggling. Sure, the story is definitely hyperbolic in the sense that the runner seemed a bit nonchalant at the sight of someone being murdered. But I do think that the perspective is real. We make bargains with ourselves and justify our non-action based on an assumption of facts that we can't prove. The runner wanted to believe that she didn't see what she saw. She wanted to return to her agenda of the day assuming that everything was going to be fine for the two quarreling and for her. Has there been a time that you felt this way too? Be honest, when you see an unhoused person on the street, you make assumptions about them and about their life choices that you use to justify why you don't help them if you could. If a couple is at a restaurant and they start to argue or even worse, one of them is verbally abusing the other. Instead of getting involved and standing up for the bullied one, we avert our eyes and say it is none of our business. Maybe you don't. If so, good for you, really and truly. We need to be more like that, be willing to get involved with strangers if they need us. Would you have stopped it, or would you have stayed hidden in the bush? I wanted to write about this because I wanted us to keep asking ourselves these questions. It is important as we grow ourselves and as a society. Stay curious about yourself.

Unexpected Moments is a poem that I wanted to write about here because, first of all, I am hoping the symbolism is clear, and second because it was so personal to me at the time that I had to call attention to it. Divorce is hard, there is no way around it. Anyone saying otherwise is fooling themselves most of all. Through the rough parts of it, the fighting, the decisions, the fighting again, it is easy to see some of the surface hurt that you go through and that you show to others. After it is all over, there is another pain that you find that you didn't know you were going to have. Not just the end of your marriage but the end of the life you thought you would have. Sitting on the porch with grandkids and waking up to each other, all of those things that you thought you would do are different now. A wash of failure and grief comes over you that you never expected. This is what I meant by this piece. In the moment, when everything is happening and you are just rolling through it, you get dinged, and things break, and you can pop out the dings and replace the glass. But when the fundamental part of yourself is bent or broken, it takes some time to realize that and even more time to heal. And sometimes you just have to get a new you, like you have to get a new car. Go shopping, do some test drives and rediscover yourself.

Heat and Lucky Number Sevens were both personal for me. Trying to put on different faces in the middle of disaster is sometimes impossible. It is, however, what we have to do sometimes.

Find a place or a person that you can be yourself, you can be safe, and you can break down. They are happy to be there for you, they will push you to grow and they will tell you the truth and they will let you cry. For as long as you need to, they will let you cry. And when you are done, they will build you up again. For everyone else, they can see the face you want to show them. All of that is up to you, but again, divorce is hard. Let it be hard because you can do hard things.

The Glow and The Golden Sword were both written in the middle of my growing up period. The Glow was representative of me finally understanding that I make my own rules. The light comes from inside me. I think that I have to find it somewhere else and put it in me – but it doesn't work that way. When you get to know yourself, respect the person you are and forgive yourself for forgetting that, you start making your own light. It draws others in and they want to learn something from you. The Golden Sword is also a bit about that forgiveness. Forgiving others for the devastation they caused and forgiving yourself for it too. Forgiveness is not for the weak. It takes strength to look someone in the face that has made a point to destroy you, hurt you, forget you – and understand that the only person's opinion of you that matters is you. God sees your heart and you know your heart, even if you hide from it. If you want to be free, forgive.

Still and Future were for my kids. They really were the glue that held me together when I was DEFINITELY falling apart. To be honest they still do, and I have been divorced for over ten years now. I had to have something good to focus on when everything else seemed to be like a meteor shower in my life crashing to the ground in a hazy boom and leaving craters all over. My kids sustained me. I am going through one of the most difficult times of my life now. I was diagnosed with breast cancer last year and I am in my second chemo cycle now and I need people more than ever. It is one of my own personal battles I had to overcome to learn to lean on others. Accepting help and allowing myself to be ok with it, those are keys for me. I am more than proud of them for everything they accomplish and for everything they learn from the shots they miss.

From the early days to the easier days, the problem was *never* the man or the job or the relationship. The problem was me. Please know that this is my opinion of my situations. I was the one that couldn't commit to an emotional vulnerability. I was the one that didn't depend on honesty to be the ultimate mediator in an argument. I was the one that put others' peace before my own. I was the one that traded my life for theirs for a time. I responded to poor behavior by acceptance instead of boundaries. I created an environment where I enabled poor behavior from others around me. Managers, family, spouses, kids…

In the really dark times when I had a "friend" that became an enemy, she once told me in a very direct and very harsh way that I was a doormat and why wouldn't people treat me that way if I kept laying down for them to drag their feet across. At the time, I was furious, of course, and went on about how we needed to cut her out of our lives…yada, yada, yada. Turns out she became the first betrayal I would have to heal from, but the thing about the doormat stuck. If I keep laying down, they will keep dragging their feet across me. Having boundaries wouldn't make me mean or rude. It is merely a show of respect for myself. A sign that I know the limits of what I can accept and what I will not. I am still not in command of my emotions enough to respond every time I am triggered with boundaries instead of emotion. But

I am getting better. In an argument, when someone says something that gets under your skin there are a couple of choices. Allow your buttons to be pushed, respond with that hurt on the edge of your tongue and then watch the whole thing spiral out of control. Or... take a breath. Remember where you draw your lines and respond with those facts. Guard your peace. That is the best thing that I have learned through the years. I had to learn how to guard my own peace. Stop letting off handed comments take away my joy and excitement and pleasure. With all the crappy things that come and go in life, that saying is so true, man it just is - "You cannot control everything that happens to you, but you can control your reaction".

Forgive, grow, love, learn, be the best version of yourself you can be.